HOW TO BE MORE CREATIVE

HOW TO BE MORE CREATIVE

by David D. Edwards

The author is indebted to the many other
authors, scientists, psychologists, educators,
designers, et al. who are cited in these pages.
This book would not exist without their efforts.

Library of Congress Catalog Card Number: 78-71652
ISBN: 0-933264-00-3

An **OP** book published by

Occasional Productions
593 Vasona Avenue
Los Gatos, CA 95030

Printed in the United States of America.

CONTENTS

"From time immemorial the gift of creativity
has been venerated almost as if it were divine."

from the preface of
The Act of Creation

IN THE BEGINNING

I first became intrigued with the subject of creativity as an architecture student more than 12 years ago. Then, I erroneously believed, you either had it or you didn't. Creativity was a gift given to a chosen few. Years later I came to question that belief and began researching the subject. I wanted to know if my creative talents as a writer, editor, painter, and occasional inventor were truly fixed quantities, or talents that could be expanded and improved. After reading more than 40 books on creativity and beginning to practice a number of basic creative principles, I found that I could and have become more creative. And I'm convinced that anyone can do the same.

This book is the result of that research and the realization of two goals: one, to challenge my personal creative abilities; and two, to show you how *you* can become more creative. If you're one of the many, many people who say with an air of resignation, "I wish I were more creative," then this book is for you. If you consider yourself to be creative already, believe me when I say there are proven techniques you can use to stretch your creativity even further. Creativity is indeed a divine gift, but one that has been given to us all.

1 ARE YOU CREATIVE?

Anybody can be creative. And anyone can be more creative than he or she is now. That's because each of us possesses inborn creative abilities that can be exercised and strengthened just like our physical abilities. Psychologists have found that creative ability is distributed more or less equally among us. They have also discovered that apparent differences in creativity are really the result of how effectively each individual uses his or her inner resources. To be more creative, they say, all we need is a basic understanding of how creativity works -- and a real desire to flex our creative muscles. The encouraging message is that you and I can easily become more creative if we simply put our minds to it.

   Actually, you are already a creative individual. As one example of your creativity, you have a vivid imagination and often invent colorful stories. These short stories are rich in symbolism, complex in plot, and filled with provocative visual imagery. And not only are you imaginative, you're prolific as well: every night you create four or five of these vignettes. That's right, every night you dream. And what could be more creative than a dream?

   From beginning to end, your dreams are imaginative pieces of pure fantasy. You create the cast of characters, you write the dialogue and direct the action; you even star in some of these late night productions. Unfortunately, not all of us remember our dreams with equal clarity, so many of these elaborate fictions remain submerged in our subconscious. But as Robert McKim points out in his book, *Experiences in Visual Thinking*, "whether you remember your dreams or not, you are imaginative, often profoundly so, for about an hour and a half every night. No one who dreams can correctly say that he is unimaginative -- and everyone dreams."[1]

In addition to being an imaginative storyteller, you're also an accomplished problem solver. You successfully solve hundreds of problems every week because that's precisely what your mind is designed to do. These aren't always momentous, earth-shaking problems but simple, everyday bread-and-butter problems that make up daily life. Cooking dinner, for example, is a problem that requires creative vision. Writing a letter is a problem that's solved with an act of the imagination. Driving your car across town is a major problem with a whole set of intricate subproblems. Most of us take driving for granted. But if you consider the matter with perspective, it's simply amazing that the human mind is capable of sifting through a blizzard of information accurately and rapidly to make all the proper decisions and responses.

Now, many of the problems we solve every day are commonplace, as are many of the solutions we employ. Opening a can of tuna is rarely an example of creative thinking. But each of these examples demonstrates a definite creative potential which we utilize, consciously or not, every day of our lives. The point is that everyone has the capacity to solve a multitude of problems, quickly and easily.

Imagination and problem solving are essential to anyone who wants to be more creative because creativity is the ability to solve problems in imaginative ways. Each of us chooses which problems will tax our personal creativity. For the creative dancer the problem may be expressing movement and emotion with the human body; for the creative designer, producing original and functional design; for the creative businessperson, achieving continual growth and profitability; for the creative comedian, making people laugh; for the creative scientist, inducing theory from observable facts.

No matter what your interests or goals, to be creative you must solve with imagination the problems you've decided are important to you. As you read through this book, consider the areas in your life in which you'd like to be more creative. There, you'll discover the problems that need to be solved creatively.

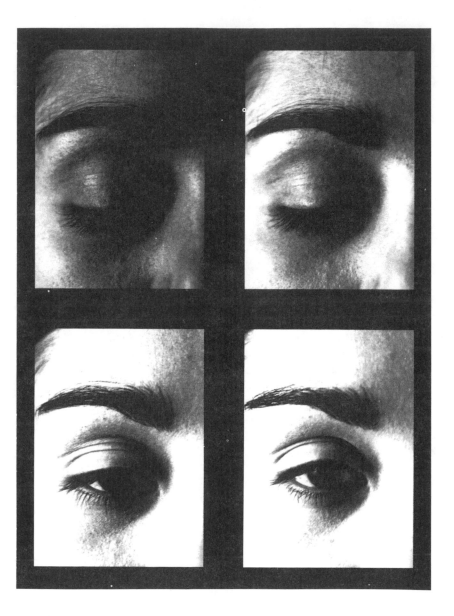

WORKSHEET 1: DREAM IMAGERY

Take a minute or two and recall a recent dream.
Summarize the action and write it here. Do you remember
sights or sounds? Was the dream imagery familiar to you
or unfamiliar? Was it realistic? What emotions do you
associate with the dream -- was it pleasurable, painful,
sexy, frightening?

WORKSHEET 1 *continued*

2 MISCONCEPTIONS

There are three common misconceptions about creativity that prevent many of us from being more creative. Each of these misconceptions is based on the mistaken belief that only the chosen few are creative. According to this theory, only the Picassos, the Edisons, and the Einsteins are creative; the rest of us are mere mortals. The unfortunate result of this type of negative thinking is to discourage the majority from having any creative aspirations at all. Few of us can realistically expect to match the achievements of the world's great minds. But the truth is, you don't have to be a genius to be creative.

Misconception #1: BEING CREATIVE MEANS BEING ARTISTIC.

Often people mistakenly equate creative ability with artistic ability. To be creative, they believe, you must paint or draw or sculpt or dance. Yet artistic creations are only one form of creativity. There are many ways in which one's creativity can be expressed. Inventors are creative, and so are cooks, architects, salespeople, mothers, fathers, and of course, children. There have been books written on *Creative Business*, *Creative Chess*, *Creative Decorating*, *Creative Electronics*,

Creative Marriage, Creative Photography, even
Creative Survival, which indicate that
creativity is not limited to a particular field
or profession.

In fact, the reverse may be true. It's
possible that a painter can be less creative
than an insurance salesman. And an auto
mechanic can be more creative than a writer.
That's because a work of art created by an
uninspired, routine formula is really less
creative than an imaginative sales campaign or
an ingenious solution to a mechanical problem.
Artistic output may be one expression of
creativity, but it's not necessary to be artistic to be creative.

Misconception #2: CREATIVITY DEMANDS GREAT SKILL.

This misconception assumes that creativity and
experience are the same thing. Actually, they
are two complementary skills. Abraham Maslow,
in his psychological analysis of creativity,
separated "the inspiration phase of creativity
from the working out and the development of the
inspiration." The latter phase, he wrote,
"relies very much on just plain hard work, on
the discipline of the individual who may spend
half a lifetime until he becomes finally ready
for a full expression of what he sees."[2]

Creativity involves technique, yes, a technique for solving problems. And creative
ability is a skill that can be learned, a mental
skill. But becoming more creative is not the

same thing as learning to paint a realistic portrait, write a novel, or design a miniaturized solar cell. It's true that greater creativity can enhance the efforts of anyone who wants to paint or write or design. But each of these achievements requires creativity *and* a learned skill. Don't discount your creative ability when you may simply need more time to pay the dues of experience.

Misconception #3: C=(f)I or CREATIVITY IS A FUNCTION OF INTELLIGENCE.

Many people think you have to be brilliant to be creative. Yet tests have shown that beyond a minimum level of intelligence, there is no correlation between intellect and creativity. The researcher who conducted the tests concluded that "Being more intelligent does not guarantee a corresponding increase in creativeness. It simply is not true that the more intelligent person is necessarily the more creative one."[3] Of course, the creative individual may be a genius on the intelligence scale, but the reverse is also quite possible: he or she may possess no more than average intellectual ability.

3 BLOCKS TO CREATIVITY

If you have this tremendous inborn capacity for
creativity, why aren't you using it more
freely? Why are children widely recognized as
being more creative than adults? One reason
is that muscles, physical or mental, atrophy
with disuse. Creativity is neither taught nor
nurtured in our schools or our society, so
it's understandable we fail to realize our full
potentials. The child in us grows old and
much of our natural creativity is ignored or
repressed.

There's another reason you're less creative
than you can be: your mind and culture conspire
against you. That's because they like conformity -- it's safer for your ego and for
society. This conspiracy involves a number of
roadblocks that keep you out of unexplored
creative fields and in the fast lane of
society's safe and sensible freeway. One of
the first and most important steps to greater
creativity is to recognize and remove these
blocks. They can take three forms: emotional,
perceptual, and cultural.

"Many of the problems associated with
creativity are in the form of emotional blocks
within one's self," wrote John E. Arnold in an
article entitled "Useful Creative Techniques."[4]
"They must be solved first before effective
and productive problem solving can take place."

Arnold, an influential leader in creative education, recognized that much of our creativity can be blocked by inner fears and self-doubts.

Emotional Block #1: FEAR.

The most common type of emotional block is fear. Fear of appearing stupid, fear of making a mistake, fear of failing. Asking questions, which is essential to creativity, means laying your ignorance out in the open. That's something we all learned to avoid a long time ago. It's still hard at times to risk ridicule or disfavor and come right out and say "I don't know."

Fear of making a mistake often paralyzes us into doing nothing. But then doing nothing may be a mistake itself. It's always better to have a dozen ideas, even if half of them are wrong, than to have no ideas at all.

Fear of failing is perhaps the biggest block of all. No one wants to fail. And some of us will go to extraordinary lengths to avoid failure of any kind. Some people won't dance for fear of failing on the dance floor. Others won't play games for fear of losing. Some of us won't quit jobs we loath because we fear failing in a new career.

But failure is a universal experience. Practically everyone fails before he or she succeeds, especially while learning a new skill. And without that failure there can be no

success. Would you have learned to walk if you
had quit after your first fall? The only real
difference between a baby learning to walk
and an adult learning to ski is that when the
adult falls down his or her *ego* gets bruised.

A willingness to take risks, especially to
risk failure, is an essential characteristic of
the creative person. Woody Allen, after
writing and directing his first non-comedy film,
told an interviewer "If you're not failing
now and again, it's a sign you're playing it
safe."

Breaking through your fears isn't easy. It
takes courage and perseverance. But if you can
allow yourself to be afraid, and yet continue,
you can take a big step towards being more
creative.

"If you're not failing now and again, it's a sign you're playing it safe."

WORKSHEET 2: FEAR·FULNESS

*Make a list of all the things you'd like to do but
don't because of fear. For example, sing, entertain
more, speak out in public, begin a conversation with
an attractive stranger, quit your job. After each,
list the type of fear that blocks you. What can you
do to overcome these fears? Are they justified? Why?*

WORKSHEET 2 *continued*

Emotional Block #2: THE NEED TO CONFORM.

Everyone has a deep need to conform, to belong to a group. We conform in our dress, our speech, our activities -- and in our thinking. But being creative often means being different, in our thoughts and in our solutions to problems. While some of us are afraid of being different, it doesn't have to mean eccentric, or oddball, or anti-social. It's simply a willingness to try new things.

   Individuals who need to conform closely to society's rules and regulations may find it difficult to be creative. That's because leaving the well-marked roadway to explore the unknown can be disorienting and uncomfortable. Expressing ideas that run counter to popular opinion means risking disapproval and censure. But to be creative, relax your need for conformity and be prepared to break the rules.

Emotional Block #3: FRUSTRATION.

We all have a frustration threshold. When it's exceeded, because of repeated failure or too much pressure, the autonomic nervous system takes over. Then our behavior is no longer controlled by our initial goal and it becomes difficult if not impossible to solve a problem creatively.

   When you're blocked by frustration, the best solution is to relax completely, physically and mentally. Then, in the next minute or the next day, begin again with a fresh attitude and perhaps a fresh approach to the problem. Efforting through the frustration will do no good. In a state of frustration the passage to your creativity is blocked, just as if there were an automatic shutoff valve.

Emotional Block #4: INAPPROPRIATE MOTIVATION.

Without sufficient motivation we don't turn on our talents. If a problem is boring or doesn't challenge our abilities, we're unlikely to discover our full creative powers. And individuals who are convinced they have no creative ability don't even try.

But surprisingly, too much motivation can also block creativity. If you're too anxious to solve a problem, you may attack it ineffectively. While concentrating on the solution, you may misunderstand the problem; pressed for results, you accept the first workable answer as the best answer; blind with enthusiasm, you overlook the obvious. As one psychologist puts it, "motivation stimulates action, which may preclude thinking."[6] Or, more simply, "the man in a hurry misses the way." (Proverbs 19).

If you find yourself attacking a problem too zealously, watch out. Slow down, back up, and give yourself the time necessary to examine all aspects of the situation. Creativity often blooms best in an environment of relaxed awareness. Excessive motivation, like frustration, can make you work too hard. And trying

Fear of criticism inhibits creative performance.

too hard creates an inner tension that blocks you from your creativity.

Emotional Block #5: A TENDENCY TO JUDGE IDEAS.

Being creative means coming up with an abundance of ideas and then evaluating which is best. Unfortunately, passing judgment seems to be one of the most enjoyable and prevalent of human habits. Confronted with a new idea, the natural tendency for many of us is to point out its flaws. The average group of people searching for new ideas will spend more time defeating ideas than conceiving them.

But judging when you should be creating blocks you from experiencing many good, but undiscovered, ideas. Creativity requires a positive outlook, not a negative, judgmental one. If you want to be more creative, suspend your judgment for awhile. There will be plenty of time to evaluate the merits of each idea later. Without stopping to judge, your creativity can generate momentum. One idea can build on another and the flow of creativity can pour forth unimpeded.

Emotional Block #6: AN INTOLERANCE FOR CHAOS.

Searching for creative ideas can be an untidy business. You need an open and receptive attitude to hold unresolved and sometimes conflicting information in your mind at the same time. This stage of the creative process can be uncomfortable. It's a state where everything is a jumble and nothing is coming clear. But, the longer you can maintain this state of unequilibrium, the longer you can prolong your creative mode of thinking. Your mind is now a bit like a kaleidoscope. The more you turn the bits of information over in your mind, the more creative possibilities you'll discover.

If you have an overriding need for orderly thinking, you may find this stage of creative thinking difficult. Psychologists call this block an inability to "defer closure." You may feel compelled to resolve the problem quickly, to wrap things up neatly with no loose ends. But this emotional need for order and resolution can block your creativity.

To be creative, allow your mind to relax, defer closure, and incubate on a problem. You must be willing to be mentally messy for a time, knowing that from the chaos creative ideas will eventually emerge.

Emotional Block #7: EGO AND SELF-SATISFACTION.

Falling in love with one of your ideas can keep you from searching for other, potentially superior, solutions. Guard against committing yourself to a good idea too soon. Of course, it's hard to temper your excitement when you get a rush of creative insight. But remember, not all sparks start fires. Healthy self-confidence in your abilities is essential, but don't get so smug that you stop looking for new and better ideas.

PERCEPTUAL OR INTELLECTUAL BLOCKS

To be creative, you must perceive a problem clearly and correctly. Perceptual or intellectual blocks involve your perceptions of a problem and how your mind goes about solving it. The best way to comprehend perceptual blocking is to experience it first-hand. So, here are three problems for you to solve.

As you work through the problems, pay particular attention to how your mind searches for solutions. If it's not convenient to do the examples now, set this book aside and do them later. Your understanding of perceptual blocking will be much greater if you can actually experience your own blocks in action.

PROBLEM #1: Attach two pieces of string to the ceiling. Each string should hang down to within 12" of the floor, but the two strings should be far enough apart that with one string in hand you can't reach the other. The problem is to tie the two strings together without removing them from the ceiling. Using other props in the room is okay. Give yourself ten minutes and find as many different solutions as you can.

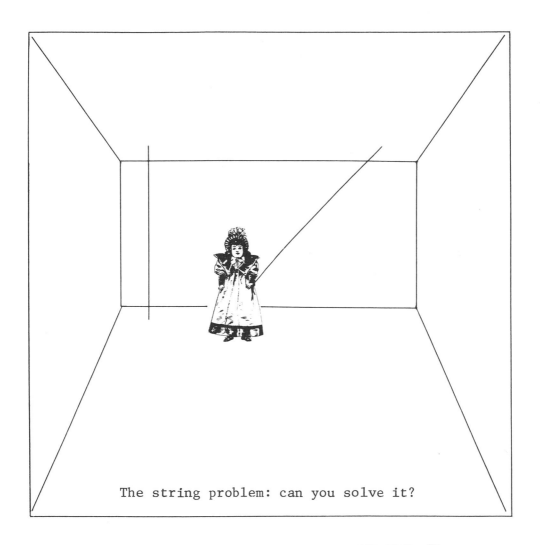

The string problem: can you solve it?

Most solutions to this problem can be classified into four categories, and each category is determined by how the problem was perceived. CATEGORY A: If you perceive the problem as *my arms are too short* then the solutions you might consider involve extending your reach: for example, a stick or pole or some object with a handle. CATEGORY B: If you perceive the problem as *the strings are too short* then your solutions might involve ways to extend the strings: tying another string to them, using a window shade cord, a belt, etc. CATEGORY C: If you perceive the problem as *one string won't stay in the middle while I reach for the other* your solutions involve ways to tie one string down, perhaps with a chair in the center. CATEGORY D: And if you perceive the problem as *the second string won't come to me while I grasp the first* then your solutions might involve opening a window to create a breeze or using a fan to blow the second string towards you, or tying a weight to the string and swinging it like a pendulum.[7]

If you perceived all four categories, you're an exceptionally flexible problem solver. If you didn't perceive all four, you've experienced perceptual blocking.

PROBLEM #2: Without lifting your pen or pencil, connect all nine dots on the opposite page with four straight lines. Allow yourself two minutes.

32

PROBLEM #3: If you didn't solve problem #2, try it now with a different set of dots.

(The answers are on page 103.)

When you first began working on problem #2, your mind may have assumed the solution was to be found within an imaginary square bounded by the outside dots. However, to solve the problem you had to go beyond the page's physical limitations, just as you had to go beyond your mind's initial perceptual limitations. If you failed to solve problem #2, then #3 should have been a bit easier simply because the dots were placed well within the borders of the page. The new arrangement gave you the clue to explore the surrounding area for a possible solution.

Perceptual Block #1: POOR PROBLEM DEFINITION.

Few people like problems. The natural tendency when confronted with a problem is to solve the thing as quickly as possible and get on to something else. The trouble with that approach is obvious: a poorly considered problem too often results in a poorly conceived solution.

   We are basically solution-minded rather than problem-minded. That means we're more likely to expend time and energy attempting to solve a problem before we're even sure what the problem is. We rush to find the answer just as students rush through an examination without

.   .   .

.   .   .

.   .   .

reading all the instructions. Sometimes, to the students' chagrin, the last line of the instructions says "Disregard all previous instructions and stop working."

Consider for a minute this mind-stopping thought:

"the desk is under the pencil"

This kind of total reversal in thinking is essential for a careful definition of the problem. Examining the situation from totally different points-of-view will clarify the problem and probably suggest totally different solutions. For example, if you find the front door of your house locked and you don't have the key, you can pick the lock -- or you can try the back door. Walking around to the back of the house is a perfect image for reversing your point-of-view. It's also a good example of careful problem definition: the problem is not that the front door is locked but that you're unable to get into the house. (You could also ring the doorbell. Who knows, maybe someone's at home?)

Perceptual Block #2: USING THE WRONG APPROACH.

Trying to solve a mathematical problem with words is cumbersome if not impossible. Trying to describe the Mona Lisa with an equation is ludicrous. Yet often our minds attempt these impossible solutions until we realize the need to use an appropriate language or strategy.

Some problems must be solved verbally, others mathematically, still others visually. Many people successfully solve certain problems with their feelings -- "what feels right" -- which is an emotional or intuitive language.

To be most creative you need to be something of a linguist. That means you must have the flexibility to employ a wide range of methods or languages to solve problems. While some people naturally seem to be more fluent than others, all you need to converse in any language is a simple vocabulary.

Here's a partial checklist of languages you can use to unblock your creativity. When confronted with a new problem, ask yourself if the problem/solution requires

- ☐ a drawing or diagram

- ☐ an equation or numbers

- ☐ words, written or spoken

- ☐ sounds, for example, music

- ☐ emotion, such as inspiration

- ☐ time

- ☐ physical change, such as movement

- ☐ logic

- ☐ intuition

By using the right language or perhaps a combination of languages (a dialect?) you'll be able to fully articulate your creativity.

Perceptual Block #3: USING INCORRECT DATA.

Anytime you try to solve a problem with faulty information, you've got problems. Computer specialists use the phrase "garbage in, garbage out," which means if your computer of a mind is working with inaccurate information, you're likely to get inaccurate answers.

If your creativity is blocked by what seems to be a square-peg-in-a-round-hole, examine all the variables of the problem carefully. One of your facts could be faulty: for example, the assumption that the solution must be made of metal, or that it's logical, or two-dimensional, or a number, or light enough to carry, etc.

Perceptual Block #4: FAILURE TO USE YOUR SENSES.

Each of the senses is a type of language for creative problem solving. Visual imagery gets a lot of attention because our sight dominates many of our perceptions. But you can also use your nose, your ears, your sense of touch, and your taste buds to solve problems. Here are two simple examples. The next time you're planning a dinner menu, close your eyes (to give your other senses a chance) and taste the dishes you're planning to prepare. Don't visualize their appearance, imagine their *taste*. Tomorrow morning before you look into your closet to decide what you'll wear, close your eyes and imagine what you'd like your clothes to *feel* like on your body.

To unblock all of your senses and to expand your creativity, ask yourself what the problem/solution looks/tastes/smells/feels/sounds like. You may be surprised by what your other senses can tell you.

Perceptual Block #5: AN INABILITY TO UTILIZE ALL OF YOUR ABILITIES.

Sometimes your mind knows the answer but you're blocked from using it. Remembering dreams is a profound example. Dream imagery is highly imaginative, vividly visual, and often poetic in its symbolism. Yet many people have difficulty consciously employing this powerful aspect of their imagination. Because of an inability to get in touch with their dream memory, part of their creativity remains blocked within the subconscious.

Creativity can also be blocked by an individual's preference for using one ability rather than another. Perhaps you're more fluent verbally than emotionally, or you prefer to use logic rather than intuition. Psychologists studying problem solving in animals have found that sources of failure depend on the behavior repertoires of each animal. Learning to pull a string to open a food box is easier for cats than dogs because cats are more likely to react to a dangling string. Pigs are more likely to solve a problem that requires raising a platform because of their rooting ability.[8]

In humans, behavior repertoires can vary from

individual to individual and between men and women. To generalize greatly, men may be more capable of solving problems that require the hand-eye coordination developed through sports. Women, on the other hand, may be more adept solving problems that require emotional sensitivity. Children skilled with words may score higher on IQ tests than children with less verbal ability.

For the most part, however, behavior repertoires are determined by our attitude towards ourselves. If a particular skill or talent doesn't fit our self-image, we don't use that talent well. In so doing we divorce ourselves from some of our inherent natural abilities. For example, creativity can be blocked by thinking *I can't*. If you say "I'm terrible at math" or "I'm not mechanically inclined" you fail to enjoy your greatest creativity simply because you aren't exercising all of your talents. Everybody can draw to some degree, but most of us will say "No, I can't draw" when even a crude drawing may be the simplest solution to a problem.

To be more creative, learn to expand your problem-solving repertoire. And be sure to exploit to their fullest the natural abilities you already possess. Be prepared to change your self-image if necessary to unblock some of your hidden talents. For example, does your present self-image really allow you to be more creative?

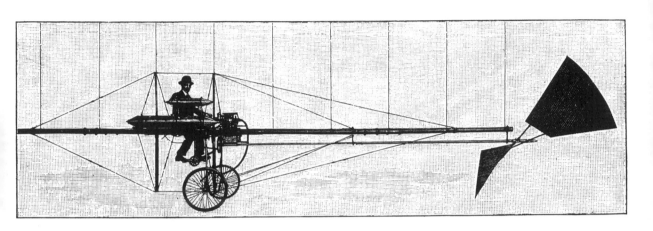

"If God had intended man to fly, He would have given him wings."

Anonymous

WORKSHEET 3: THE POWER OF NEGATIVE THINKING

Make an I can't list -- things, in your opinion, you can't do. Then, consider each item to decide if you have absolutely no talent, or simply less than you'd like. Finally, list one contradiction for each I can't: for example, "I can't handle math. But every year I do my own income tax return."

WORKSHEET 3 *continued*

CULTURAL BLOCKS

Cultural blocks are caused by attitudes in society and among our peers that inhibit creativity. These attitudes block us from creative possibilities by constantly telling us what is right and what is wrong, what is possible and what isn't. Sometimes these cultural blocks are so much a part of our upbringing that we're blind to their role as barriers to greater creativity.

James Adams, a Stanford design professor and author of *Conceptual Blockbusting*, notes that projects requiring his students to break through cultural blocks are among the most popular, since the blocks can be so difficult to overcome and yet so obvious once they're discovered. One problem, for example, required removing a dollar bill from beneath a carefully balanced object without tipping the object over. The solution, which many of the students never perceived because of our society's attitude about money, was to tear the bill in half. Another problem could only be solved by destroying one playing card in a deck of 52. A third project involved moving certain pieces around a board in a given sequence. It turned out to be impossible to follow the rules and solve the problem. The cultural block? -- following the rules.[9]

Cultural Block #1: "NOW, LET'S BE LOGICAL."

Rational, logical, linear thinking is top dog

in our society. Intuition, feelings, and non-linear modes of thinking are underdogs. We are continually encouraged to be logical and discouraged from being irrational. When someone becomes emotionally upset, a common admonition is "now, now, let's be logical about this..." But actually, under emotional stress the rational mind can short-circuit and you can experience a flash of irrational inspiration. If you've ever had a hunch or feeling, and the courage to act upon it, you know the value of your own intuition.

Recent research has shown that rational, linear thinking is controlled by the left side of the brain, while certain aspects of creativity are controlled by the right side. In an article in *Learning* magazine entitled "Are You Teaching Only One Side of the Brain?" Robert E. Samples summarized these findings by writing: "The left cerebral hemisphere tends to process information in a reductive or sorting out way in order to find the best answer or solution. The right side functions on relationships and multiple-images, tends to multiply affiliated ideas and mix pictures, images, experiences, emotions, etc. in a way that encourages invention. It thrives on invention."[10]

While alternative modes of thinking are vastly underrated in our society, they can be useful tools for achieving greater creativity. To help break through this cultural block, keep in mind that 1: Logic can solve problems, but creativity often requires a leap of the imagin-

ation; 2: Creative ideas often don't make any sense; and 3: An illogical idea may not be a bad idea.

Cultural Block #2: ROLE STEREOTYPING.

The assumption that gender determines our abilities, such as the ability to fix an appliance or to raise children, is an example of a cultural block that's been exposed and brought within our collective consciousness. Because of changes in society, women and men can now explore new roles that were blocked before.

Another common cultural block is the assumption that people without the advantages of advanced training, higher education, or superior intelligence are incapable of coming up with good ideas. For example, you may discount your own abilities or those of others simply because of a lack of credentials. If so, your cultural values are blocking you. It's not necessary to have a degree or years of experience to be creative.

Cultural Block #3: PLAYING IS FOR KIDS.

In the vernacular of our society, children can play but adults spend leisure hours relaxing or enjoying various recreational activities. As adults we're expected to grow up and put childish things like play behind us. That's unfortunate because being creative means being willing and able to play: with ideas, materials,

48

and reality. Creativity is a kind of mental play. To be more creative, relax your grown-up inhibitions and let your mind out to play more often.

Cultural Block #4: FANTASY AND DAYDREAMS ARE BAD

Early in life, society taught us that too many fantasies can be a symptom of maladjustment. Daydreaming, on the other hand, is simply un-productive -- and therefore, probably a sin. Both activities suffer poor reputations and most adults don't cultivate either as habits.

And yet much creative thinking can spring from reverie and quiet, unproductive moods that are divorced from reality. "The dynamic prin-ciple of fantasy is play," wrote Carl Jung, "which belongs also to the child, and...appears to be inconsistent with the principle of serious work. But without this playing with fantasy, no creative work has ever yet come to birth."

Breaking through this block won't be easy, but if you can daydream and fantasize without feeling guilty, terrific. If you can't, strive for it.

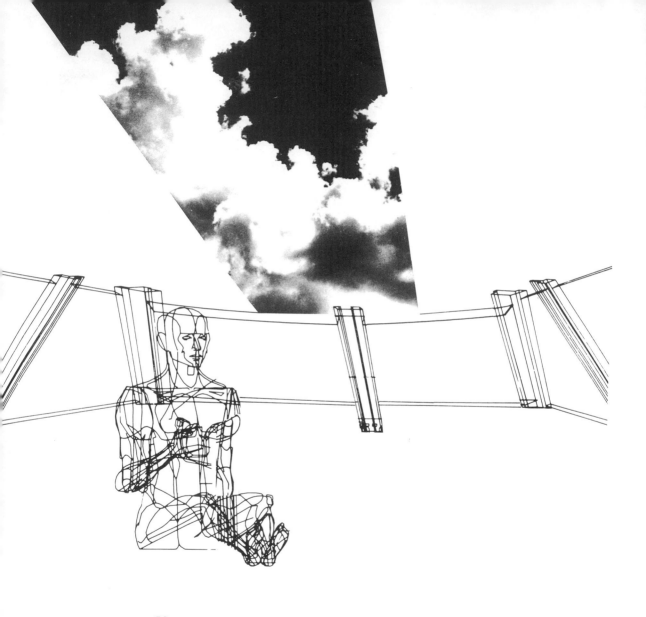

WORKSHEET 4: MY DREAM ROOM

*Imagine a room or space that is entirely your own,
equipped and furnished any way you please. It's a
private place which no one will see or enter unless you
invite them inside. Close your eyes and take as long as
you like to imagine this space. Then write down what
you've created.*

WORKSHEET 4 *continued*

Cultural Block #5: "THOU SHALT TRY NOTHING NEW."

Of course, no one says that aloud. But it's the great unspoken commandment that directs many of our thoughts and actions. Tradition and the status quo are known, liked, and comfortable; change is unknown, disliked, and anxiety-producing -- and almost always resisted, either by the individual or by society. While change for the sake of change is rarely creative, the creative individual is always open to new ideas. This block may be one of the easiest to overcome, within your own mind. The battle is overcoming external obstacles and convincing others that your ideas have validity.

Becoming aware of blocks to your creativity is the first step towards removing them. Awareness itself may be all that's necessary to free your thinking. Other times barriers can persist despite your best efforts to overcome them. No one can realistically expect to remove all the blocks, but you can go a long way towards minimizing their impact.

  As you read the second half of this book, you'll find specific strategies that can help you break through creative blocks. Several books listed in the bibliography on page 104 contain effective blockbusting exercises. Review the checklist on the following page occasionally to discover which blocks continue to give you trouble.

EMOTIONAL BLOCKS

- ☐ Fear.
- ☐ The need to conform.
- ☐ Frustration.
- ☐ Inappropriate motivation.
- ☐ Tendency to judge rather than create ideas.
- ☐ An intolerance for chaos.
- ☐ Ego and self-satisfaction.

PERCEPTUAL BLOCKS

- ☐ Poor problem definition.
- ☐ Using the wrong approach.
- ☐ Using incorrect data.
- ☐ Failure to use your senses.
- ☐ Inability to utilize all of your abilities.

CULTURAL BLOCKS

- ☐ "Now, let's be logical."
- ☐ Role stereotyping.
- ☐ Playing is for kids.
- ☐ Fantasy and daydreams are bad.
- ☐ "Thou shalt try nothing new."

detail from Picasso's *Child Sitting in a Chair*

"Ah, good taste! What a
 dreadful thing. Taste is the
 enemy of creativeness."

                Pablo Picasso

"Puff, puff, chug, chug,
 went the Little Blue Engine.
 'I think I can -- I think I can --
 I think I can -- I think I can.'"

The Little Engine That Could
as told by Watty Piper

4 THE CREATIVE ATTITUDE

Recognizing and removing emotional, perceptual, and cultural blocks is a giant step towards greater creativity. Once you've cleared the obstacles you can begin to establish a frame of mind that's conducive to creative thinking. That doesn't mean you simply flip a mental switch and suddenly become more creative. You can, however, create in your mind an atmosphere favorable to creative activity. "There's no magic formula for creativity," says Fredelle Maynard in her book, *Guiding Your Child to a More Creative Life*. "It's possible, though, to make suggestions about the kind of environment in which creative impulses are most likely to flower."[11]

Step #1: ESTABLISH A POSITIVE MIND-SET.

To achieve a creative attitude, begin by asserting the simple statement "I am creative." Affirming your own creative ability will minimize debilitating self-doubts and create a positive mind-set that's an essential aspect of the creative attitude. Experiments have shown the mere suggestion that a person is an original thinker improves his or her creative ability. Participants who were told they had a reputation for being creative showed a definite improvement in their problem-solving ability, with a significant increase in imaginative ideas.[12] In other words, if you think you're creative, you are.

To become more creative, begin thinking of yourself as a creative person. When you assert (and believe) the simple statement "I am creative," you immediately improve your creative ability.

Step #2: LEARN TO RELAX.

A relaxed but attentive attitude is an essential characteristic of the creative mind. Being physically tense or mentally uptight is a crippling liability. Trying too hard to solve a problem only moves you farther from the solution, making it even more difficult to grasp. And concentrating too intensely can block you completely. Creative ideas must be allowed to emerge; they cannot be forced.

An absence of rigidity is an important attribute of the creative attitude. Flexibility in your approach to a problem will result in a better problem definition; flexibility in your solutions to the problem will result in a better variety of ideas. To be creative, stay loose. "If you try to be rational and controlled and orderly in this first stage of the process, you'll never get to it," says Maslow.[13]

Step #3: SUSPEND YOUR JUDGMENT FOR AWHILE.

Criticism and evaluation inhibit creative thinking. When you hear yourself say to someone "that's a good idea, but...." you're inhibiting his or her creativity and your own. When you say to yourself "that's no good, that will never work...." you're guilty of judging too soon. Give your imagination the green light and let the ideas flow. Later, there's plenty of time to turn on the red light (your judgment) and evaluate the ideas you've created.

Step #4: OPEN YOUR AWARENESS AND PERCEPTIONS.

The creative attitude is a questioning, searching state of mind. "Questioning is basic and fundamental," says Arnold. "The creative process starts with a question."[14] To be creative, you must be sensitive to problems and their implications. And while your judgment may be temporarily suspended, your analytical abilities are not. Creativity requires the ability to analyze problems and break them down into manageable components.

To achieve a creative attitude, open up your senses. Strive for a state of heightened awareness which is that fluid state of mind and body when your perceptions are sharp, responsive, and *on*. Plug into your sensory circuits and you'll maximize your creative power. "Originality," said Woodrow Wilson, "is simply a fresh pair of eyes."

WORKSHEET 5:   WHAT IS THE PROBLEM?

*This exercise is designed to test your problem
sensitivity. Look over the scene on the opposite page
and write down all possible explanations, probable and
improbable, for what's happening. Be perceptive and
imaginative in your answers.*

WORKSHEET 5 *continued*

Step #5: BECOME RECEPTIVE TO YOUR RHYTHMS.

Imagine your mind is a radio with multiple wavelengths. To be creative, you need to tune in your creative frequency. At times this fine tuning isn't easy because the sounds can be faint and indistinct. But cock your mind's ear and listen carefully. Intuition can be an important tool to greater creativity. Begin to trust your instincts and your hunches. Often you know more than you think you know.

 Tuning in also means becoming aware of your creative rhythms. Each of us has certain times of the day (and if you believe in biorhythms, times of the month) when our minds are sharp and resourceful. At other times all the efforting in the world may not produce the creative ideas we're searching for. Then, too, certain tasks can require some warm-up time while you become familiar with the problem. This warming up may take an hour or a matter of days. Learn to take advantage of this natural ebb and flow in your creative ability. Become sensitive to to your inner rhythms and when your creative energy is on full power, make the most of it.

Step #6: GIVE YOURSELF PERMISSION TO BE CREATIVE

Learning to relax is part of it. Suspending your judgment is too. But to be creative, consciously give yourself permission to be crazy, playful, outrageous. "Don't be afraid of being silly -- silliness is a sign that you are thinking creatively, because you have overcome some inhibitions in your mind." That's the advice of Werner Kirst and Ulrich Diekmeyer, authors of *Creativity Training: Become Creative in 30 Minutes a Day*.[15]

To be creative, you need a sense of psychological safety. That means no matter how ridiculous, bizarre, or silly you may appear, to yourself or to others, you have accepted your own self-worth. The sense of safety that results from this non-judgmental attitude allows you and others to act more spontaneously and with less rigidity.[16]

To give your creativity free rein, work in an environment where there's no internal or external evaluation. No criticism, no comments, no second guessing. The creative attitude requires a full measure of spontaneity, so let yourself go.

"Nothing encourages creativity like the chance to fall flat on one's face."

James D. Finley

The creative attitude allows you to establish a mental environment in which your creativity can flourish. Conditions which foster this state of mind are:

- ☐ a positive mind-set
- ☐ willing suspension of judgment
- ☐ sensitivity and awareness
- ☐ openness to experience
- ☐ flexibility
- ☐ a sense of psychological safety
- ☐ absence of evaluation and criticism
- ☐ quiet, relaxing times

Conditions which inhibit creativity include:

- ☐ doubts
- ☐ judgmental attitudes
- ☐ tight control
- ☐ pressure
- ☐ anxiety
- ☐ excessive motivation

"Creativity is so delicate a
 flower that praise tends to make
 it bloom while discouragement
 often nips it in the bud."

Alex F. Osborn

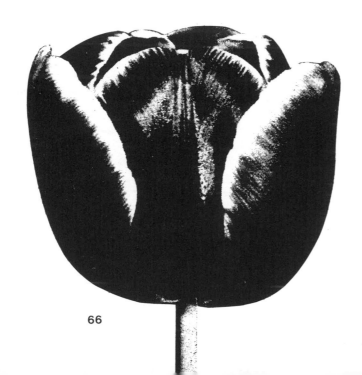

WORKSHEET 6: TAKING INVENTORY

List all the attributes you possess that make you creative. In a second column, list traits that prevent you from being more creative. What stimulates your creativity? When have you been creative in the past? What inhibits your creativity? Why?

WORKSHEET 6 *continued*

5 HOW TO CREATE IDEAS

Creativity is the ability to solve problems in imaginative ways. And while we all solve problems every day of our lives, often our solutions are unimaginative and routine. The question is, how do we develop creative ideas?

The search for new ideas involves five steps:

1. Define the problem.
2. Assemble all the information.
3. Ideate many solutions.
4. Incubate, rest, and relax.
5. Evaluate which idea is best.

1. The importance of carefully defining the problem can't be overemphasized. Too many problems are poorly solved because the problem was never made clear at the beginning. Poor problem definition is a perceptual block to creative ideas. 2. Assembling relevant information is a straight-forward process. Of course, the data you gather must be correct or you'll be creating another perceptual block: using incorrect information to solve a problem. 3. Ideating means conceiving and imagining solutions to the problem. This is where most creative thinking takes place. It's also the step that offers the greatest potential for improving your creative abilities. 4. Incubation is an important but optional step that may be by-passed during the problem-solving process

if time is unavailable. Some situations seem
to demand immediate solution. Given the time,
however, incubation is an effective tool.
5. Evaluating which idea is best must always
remain the last step in the process. Judging
your ideas as you conceive them weakens your
creative efforts.

To improve your ability to *ideate many solutions,* you can let your mind randomly select an
approach to the problem, or you can consciously
choose a strategy. Here are 12 ideating techniques that can be used to expand your creativity. Use each strategy separately or in tandem
with others. Some problems may be solved best
with several techniques; others may require only
one.

Technique #1: ORGANIZE.

Planning is a popular technique for producing
ideas. Analyzing a problem and breaking it
down into related subproblems is often an effective way to proceed. The process is thorough,
orderly, and logical. Logic can be an exceptionally powerful method for creating ideas.
The danger lies in relying exclusively on
logical thinking.

Technique #2: MAKE A LIST.

The advantage of list-making is that one idea
naturally leads to another. Afterwards you have
a written record that can be reviewed by you

70

or others. Perhaps the second or third time through the list a word or phrase will suddenly spark your thinking in a new and creative direction.

The list can be a collection of possible solutions, or a list of attributes relating to the problem. For example, let's say your problem is to develop all possible uses for a sheet of 8-1/2 x 11" typing paper. The technique of attribute listing notes the paper's

1. straight edges
2. color
3. porosity
4. right angles
5. dimensions
6. flexibility
7. flammability
8. foldability

Each of these listed attributes can lead to a potential use and possible solution to the problem.

Technique #3: FREE ASSOCIATE.

List-making can be logical and orderly or random and associative. The mind has the capacity to leap from one subject to another with amazing speed. These leaps may seem random, but actually the subjects are linked by something they share in common. The subconscious mind often makes connections that the conscious mind is unable to perceive. Learn to exploit this natural associative ability.

"An idea is a feat of association."

Robert Frost

Free associate beginning with the word mother. *Simply write down the first thing that comes to mind and continue as quickly as possible through ten entries. Then, begin again with the word* father. *Is there a cluster of meaning in the lists that reflects your attitudes towards each word. You can also free associate visually, without words. Spend a few minutes associating images, beginning with the color blue.*

WORKSHEET 7 *continued*

Technique #4: USE A CHECKLIST.

A number of experts on creativity have suggested thinking strategies or checklists for developing new ideas. The key feature of each checklist is a listing of manipulative verbs, such as

Display	Compare	Eliminate
Question	Expand	Itemize
Reverse	Freeze	Color

To demonstrate how you can use these manipulative verbs, let's say you need to prepare an original presentation for a small group. You can use the checklist like this:

Display: use visual aids, drawings, photographs, a film; build a scale model; bring actual samples....

Question: turn the presentation into an interview with group members questioning you; or make your presentation a series of questions which the group answers, creating the give-and-take of a verbal questionnaire....

Reverse: begin by asking the group what type of presentation they expect or would like to experience. Then, create a program that fulfills their expectations.

Alex Osborn, an influential leader in the study of creativity, suggested the following checklist for new ideas in his book, *Applied Imagination*:[17]

1. Put to other uses?
2. Adapt?

3. Modify?
4. Magnify?
5. Minify?
6. Substitute?
7. Rearrange?
8. Reverse?
9. Combine?

An effective way to deal with these checklists is to put each verb on a separate 3x5 card. When you want to apply the technique, flip through the cards slowly. Better yet, instead of copying these lists or others, make up your own. The principle of manipulative verbs is the basis of the technique, not the specific verbs you find on someone else's checklist.

Technique #5: FORCE CONNECTIONS.

Here's an example of forced connections suggested by Don Koberg and Jim Bagnall in *The Universal Traveler*: List all the attributes of the situation horizontally on a sheet of paper. Below each attribute, write down as many alternatives as you can think of. Then, make random runs through the different alternatives, picking one from each column. This forces new and creative combinations.[18] For example, if you want to design an original type of living environment, here are some of the basic attributes that can be manipulated:

material	size	location	shape
wood	40x40	in the hills	rectangular
paper	15x100	on the beach	circular
fiberglass	5x700	on the water	cube
cardboard	2-level	in the air	pyramid
foam	34-level	underground	spherical

Can you imagine a cardboard house in the shape of a giant slide carousel floating on the water? You've got the idea.

   Another type of forced connection involves fitting elements together that seem to have no connection whatsoever. The next time you're in the midst of solving a problem, walk into the next room and look around for a few minutes. Find one item you like -- it could be a can opener, a book binding, a photo of an eagle, whatever. Bring it back with you. Then contemplate how that object is like or unlike the problem you're considering. What about the admired object can be applied to the work at hand? These kind of forced connections do work. "How is a chameleon like a roof?" may sound like an impossible riddle. But a design group forced a connection between the chameleon's skin and the roof's surface to develop a new type of roofing material that changes color from light to dark, thereby saving energy.

Random combinations create new possibilities.

WORKSHEET 8: MAKING CONNECTIONS

What are possible connections between a light bulb and a moth? A telephone and a piece of paper? A bikini and a briefcase? A blue sky and a crayon? Go beyond the obvious and list as many connections as you can find (at least ten). Are there any relationships among the four sets of examples?

WORKSHEET 8 *continued*

Technique #6: BRAINSTORM.

The concept of brainstorming is another creative contribution made by Alex Osborn. The idea can be used by one person or a group and offers the potential of developing a tremendous number of ideas in a short time. There are four basic principles: 1) Defer judgment; no criticism is allowed, of other ideas or your own; 2) Quantity of ideas is emphasized; the more ideas in a specific length of time the better; 3) The wildest, craziest, silliest ideas are the goal; don't play it safe and conservative when you brainstorm; 4) Building upon other ideas is encouraged; that means you can piggyback one idea on another, adapt two previous ideas, recombine them, etc. To brainstorm effectively, you need a specific problem and anywhere from 15 to 90 minutes. If you brainstorm in a group, six to seven members is the optimum number. But there's no reason a large group of 100 or more can't brainstorm also.

When I was studying architecture at Iowa State, my design professor kept saying "the first solution is rarely the best solution." Scientific tests prove his advice to be right: the first half of ideas created in a prolonged effort were compared to those from the second half -- and the latter contained 78% more good ideas.[19] So, to make brainstorming work, keep thinking. The best idea may be the next idea.

WORKSHEET 9:   AN ABUNDANCE OF IDEAS

To brainstorm effectively you need an abundance of ideas. That requires fluency in your thinking. Imagine your company, or your family, has a surplus of 2 million ping pong balls. You're expected to ideate at least 50 possible uses. What can you do with 2,000,000 little white balls?

idea idea idea idea idea

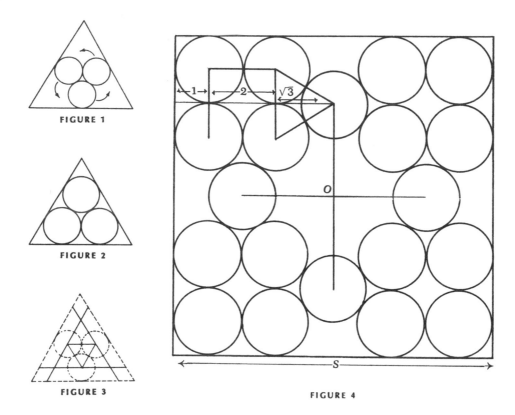

FIGURE 1

FIGURE 2

FIGURE 3

FIGURE 4

WORKSHEET 10: A VARIETY OF IDEAS

Creativity requires both fluency and **flexibility** *in your thinking. Go over your list in the previous exercise and note the number of ideas in different categories; for example: five game ideas; three floatation ideas; six uses as containers, etc. Can you conceive more uses that offer a greater variety of ideas? Expand your thinking.*

WORKSHEET 10 *continued*

Technique #7: NON-VERBALIZE.

Sometimes words can get in the way. So try solving the problem with no words allowed. Your mind will use various forms of imagery such as visual, auditory, kinesthetic, without the necessity of verbal communication. "New ideas," says Edward de Bono in his book, *New Think*, "tend to occur much more often to those who are able to escape from the rigidity of words and classifications." That's because words can be called ideas in a state of suspended animation. As soon as you commit an idea to verbal expression you fit it into a mold or suspend its animation. "Too early expression may commit an idea to a pattern of development it may not naturally have followed," says de Bono.[20]

Technique #8: SKETCH OR DOODLE.

An excellent way to ideate without words is to pick up a pencil. You don't have to possess exceptional drawing ability to be able to use this technique. The sketches you make are for yourself only and may never be shown to anyone. Don't judge them for their artistic merit; use them as tools for producing new ideas. Almost everybody doodles at one time or another. If you can doodle, you can think visually with a pen.

ink drawing by Picasso

88

WORKSHEET 11: DOODLING IS DRAWING

On a piece of plain white paper, trace the drawing on page 88 with a soft lead pencil. Then trace the figures below with a fountain or ballpoint pen. Now, turn the page and draw them again, without tracing. Try both left and right hands. The idea here is to do it, not think about it. Be loose and have some fun.

sketches by Franz Kafka

Technique #9: FEEL THE SOLUTION.

When I need a new idea, sometimes I close my eyes and ask myself, "what does it feel like?" Visceral solutions can be creative solutions. Artists and designers often times *feel* one solution is superior to another. In many instances, the reason is subjective, but creative solutions are often subjective.

An interesting study conducted several years ago showed a clear tendency for creative men to score higher in femininity than their less creative colleagues. The scores suggest that "the more creative a man is the more he reveals an openness to his own feelings and emotions, a sensitive intellect and understanding self-awareness, and wide-ranging interests, including many which in the American culture are thought of as feminine."[21]

Of course, this doesn't mean that women are necessarily more creative than men. But individuals who can draw upon all aspects of their personality -- masculine and feminine, intuitive and logical, playful and serious -- are generally more creative.

Technique #10: COMMUNICATE WITH THE UNCONSCIOUS.

The subconscious mind is filled with creative possibilities. Unfortunately, our subconscious remains well guarded much of the time. There are several ways to tap this creative wellspring. One is to get in touch with your dreams. Not only are dreams a marvelous source of novel imagery, they contain answers to many of our daily problems as well. Dreams are also recognized as the source of many creative ideas; the number of inventions and discoveries first revealed during dreams is well documented.

Another way to catch the subconscious at unguarded moments is to become more aware of thoughts and imagery when you are half asleep or fatigued. During these times of transition from a conscious to an unconscious state you can often catch glimpses of the unconscious cinema. When you wake up in the morning, lie quietly for a few minutes with your eyes closed. In a relaxed yet attentive manner, recall one of the dreams you had during the night. Similarly, as you fall asleep, attend whatever imagery or hallucinations your mind projects as you drift into that no man's land between wakefulness and sleep.

Technique #11: PLAY.

You don't need to learn how to play. You just need to relax some of the controls you live with all day. Fashion designer Bonnie Cashin tells how she has used play to generate new ideas. "Sometimes I'll take everything out of the closets, throw them on the floor, try on certain things, maybe upside down or wrong things together, and all of a sudden a certain juxtaposition looks absolutely marvelous. And thus may start a whole trend of new designs.

It's an accident; yet I wonder if the accident was meant to be. Free associations, free experiment: it's all part of the play thing."[22]

Technique #12: DO NOTHING.

In terms of the relationship between energy or cost expended (none) and the benefits (possible) this is always an option to be considered seriously. This idea of doing nothing as a deliberate course of action is the thesis of Charles Jencks and Nathan Silver in their book, *Adhocism: The Case for Improvisation*. Who knows, perhaps the problem isn't worth the time it takes to solve it. Or, the problem may be solved best when it's re-defined as a non-problem.

A few final words about incubation: Once you've completely saturated yourself with a problem and have reached an impasse, drop it altogether. Go for a walk, go fishing, go to a movie, forget it. What you're doing, of course, is putting your subconscious mind to work on the problem. There is truth to the cliche "let me sleep on it." The time your subconscious needs to deliver a solution may vary from an hour to weeks. The danger lies in relying too heavily upon this type of inspired solution and skipping all the heavy mental work beforehand. Inspiration favors the prepared mind. Recognize the power of incubation, but use it properly. It's only the lazy thinker who sits and waits for the flash of genius that may never come.

A dream image seen with the conscious eye.

6 AIDS TO CREATIVITY

There are a number of aids to creativity that can be used to supplement and support your commitment to become more creative. Here are four that can be beneficial. Consider them seriously and give each a try. They may not be for you, but then none is expensive, illegal, or dangerous to your health.

Aid #1: A DREAM DIARY.

If you have difficulty remembering your dreams, a dream diary can help. And if you do recall your dreams, the discipline of making daily entries will clarify certain images, patterns, and symbols.

   Before I began to keep a dream diary, I remembered only five or six dreams a year. When I make regular entries in my diary, I can generally recall one or two dreams every morning. Getting in touch with your dreams can be a provocative visual experience. It can also give you a greater sense of wholeness because your conscious mind can communicate more freely with your subconscious. You can discover solutions to present problems, as well as problems you didn't even know concerned you.

   To begin a dream diary, follow the guidelines listed on the next page.

1. Keep your diary or tape recorder handy.
2. Date your entry in advance. This
   symbolizes your commitment to recall
   your dreams.
3. Encourage your dreams by self-suggestion.
   Tell yourself before you fall asleep
   that you will dream that night and will
   recall the dream when you awake.
4. Record the dream immediately upon waking.
   Don't wait even minutes or the dream
   will begin slipping into the subconscious.
5. Never dismiss a dream as too trivial.
6. Record each dream as fully as possible.
   All the details may not seem to be important at the time, but they may yield
   insights later.
7. Relate your dreams to events of the day.
   This will help you analyze the "how and
   why" of your dreams.

If you're interested in dream power, do some
reading on the subject. Try *The Dream Game* by
Ann Faraday, *Creative Dreaming* by Patricia Gar-
field, or *The Dream Theater* by Faye Hammel and
Daniel Marshall. Even if you find no other
benefits, at least your dreams will demonstrate
first-hand your own creative potential.

Aid #2: RELAXATION TECHNIQUES.

Learning to relax your body and your mind has
two possible benefits: you can enhance your
creativity and improve your health. People who

practice Transcendental Meditation report one of its many benefits is an increase in creativity. A slightly different form of meditation called the Relaxation Response offers many of the same benefits, but can be practiced without the introductory lectures required by TM. To practice the Relaxation Response:

1. Sit comfortably in a quiet place.
2. Close your eyes.
3. Relax all your muscles, beginning with your toes and working slowly up to your head.
4. Breathe easily through your nose; become aware of the rhythm of your breathing.
5. As you breathe out, repeat a single word such as the word *one*.
6. Continue this for 10 or 20 minutes; afterwards, sit quietly for a few minutes, and then open your eyes.
7. Practice the technique once or twice daily, except right after eating.

People who have begun to meditate say they are less anxious and more directed in their daily activities. When they're able to relax, they're much more receptive to creative thinking.

If Transcendental Meditation or the Relaxation Response interests you, do some additional reading. The basic directions repeated here are not meant to instruct, but to show you how simple and easy the technique can be. *The Relaxation Response* by Herbert Benson is a fine introduction to the subject.

Aid #3: GUIDED FANTASY.

The ability to fantasize is an aid to creativity that can be encouraged in a number of ways. One effective stimulus is to participate in guided or directed fantasy. This can be done alone or in groups; either way the results can be astonishing. Participants put themselves in a relaxed and receptive frame of mind, with their eyes closed. Then the group leader slowly reads a series of fantasy stimuli. Within his or her own mind each individual uses the suggested images to create a personal fantasy that takes on a life of its own, much like a waking dream. After the fantasy is completed, 10 or 20 minutes later, it's instructive to share and compare each person's dream.

Basically, guided fantasy is a game of "let's pretend." Unlike six and seven-year-olds who may fantasize about princesses and monsters, adults can use the power of fantasy to gain a new perception of personal relationships, life goals, and recurrent problems. *Put Your Mother on the Ceiling* by Richard de Mille includes a variety of mind-expanding directed fantasies. Although written primarily for children, adults can play and learn from the exercises, too. McKim's book, *Experiences in Visual Thinking*, also contains several fantasy games well worth trying.

Aid #4: ADDITIONAL READING.

While this book offers an overview of the available literature, there's a tremendous amount of material that has been published on creativity. Anyone who reads and practices the ideas included here can become more creative. But the more reading and research you do, the better your knowledge and potential for even greater creativity. If you are committed to becoming more creative, check the following recommended reading. There's a complete bibliography on page 104, but these books represent the best in readability and effectiveness.

1. *Conceptual Blockbusting*, Adams
2. *A Source Book for Creative Thinking*, Parnes and Harding
3. *Problem Solving and Creativity in Individuals and Groups*, Maier
4. *Creativity Training: Become Creative in 30 Minutes a Day*, Kirst and Diekmeyer
5. *New Think*, de Bono
6. *Experiences in Visual Thinking*, McKim
7. *The Five-Day Course in Thinking*, de Bono
8. *The Practice of Creativity*, Prince
9. *Adhocism: The Case for Improvisation*, Jencks and Silver
10. *The Universal Traveler*, Koberg and Bagnall
11. *60 Seconds to Mind Expansion*, Cook and Davitz

NOTES

1 Robert McKim, *Experiences in Visual Thinking*, Brooks/Cole Publishing, 1972. pp. 25 and 83

2 Abraham Maslow, "The Creative Attitude," *Explorations in Creativity*, Harper & Row, 1967. p. 44

3 Donald F. MacKinnon, quoted by Fredelle Maynard in *Guiding Your Child to a More Creative Life*, Doubleday, 1973. p. 14

4 John E. Arnold, "Useful Creative Techniques," *A Source Book for Creative Thinking*, Scribner's, 1962. p. 253

5 Norman R. Maier, *Problem Solving & Creativity in Individuals and Groups*, Brooks/Cole Publishing, 1970. p. 177

6 Maier, p. 187

7 Maier, p. 78

8 Maier, p. 130

9 James L. Adams, *Conceptual Blockbusting*, W.H. Freeman, 1974, p. 42

10 Robert E. Samples, "Are You Teaching Only One Side of the Brain?" *Learning* magazine, February, 1975.

11 Fredelle Maynard, *Guiding Your Child to a More Creative Life,* Doubleday, 1973. p. 21

12 Maier, p. 89

13 Maslow, p. 102

14 John E. Arnold, "Education for Innovation," *A Source Book for Creative Thinking*, Scribner's, 1962. p. 130

15 Werner Kirst and Ulrich Diekmeyer, *Creativity Training: Become Creative in 30 Minutes a Day*, Wyden, 1973. p. 70

16 Carl Rogers, "Toward a Theory of Creativity," *A Source Book for Creative Thinking*, Scribner's, 1962. pp. 64-71

17 Alex F. Osborn, *Applied Imagination*, Scribner's, 1957.
18 Don Koberg and Jim Bagnall, *The Universal Traveler*,
    William Kaufmann, 1974. p. 72
19 Osborn, p. 132
20 Edward de Bono, *New Think*, Basic Books, 1967.
    pp. 83 and 100
21 Donald F. MacKinnon, *Creativity and Learning*, Houghton
    Mifflin, 1967. p. 29
22 Bonnie Cashin, quoted in *The Creative Experience*,
    Grossman Publishers, 1970. p. 244

*The author gratefully thanks those publishers who
granted permission to quote previously copyrighted
material.*

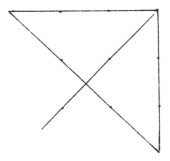

The solution to problems
2 and 3 on page 33 and 35.

BIBLIOGRAPHY

Abrams, George J. *How I Made a Million Dollars With Ideas*. Playboy, 1975.

Adams, James L. *Conceptual Blockbusting*. W.H. Freeman, 1974.

Anderson, Harold H. ed. *Creativity and Its Cultivation*. Harper & Row, 1959.

Benson, Herbert. *The Relaxation Response*. Morrow, 1975.

Cantin, Donald W. *Turn Your Ideas Into Money*. Hawthorn, 1972.

Cook, Harold and Davitz, Joel. *60 Seconds to Mind Expansion*. Random House, 1975.

De Bono, Edward. *The Five-Day Course in Thinking*. Basic Books, 1967.

De Bono, Edward. *Lateral Thinking*. Harper & Row, 1970.

De Bono, Edward. *New Think*. Basic Books, 1967.

De Mille, Richard. *Put Your Mother on the Ceiling*. Walker, 1955.

DiCyan, Erwin. *Creativity: Road to Self-Discovery*. Jove, 1978.

Faraday, Ann. *The Dream Game*. Harper & Row, 1974.

Faraday, Ann. *Dream Power*. Berkley Medallion Books, 1973.

Hammel, Faye and Marshall, Daniel. *The Dream Theater*. Harper & Row, 1978.

Harding, Rosamond. *An Anatomy of Inspiration*. Barnes & Noble, 1967.

Jackson, K.F. *The Art of Solving Problems*. St. Martin's Press, 1975.

Jencks, Charles and Silver, Nathan. *Adhocism: The Case for Improvisation*. Doubleday, 1972.

Kagan, Jerome. ed. *Creativity and Learning*. Houghton Mifflin, 1967.

Kirst, Werner and Diekmeyer, Ulrich. *Creativity Training: Become Creative in 30 Minutes a Day*. Wyden, 1973.

Koberg, Don and Bagnall, Jim. *The Universal Traveler*. William Kaufmann, 1974.

Koestler, Arthur. *The Act of Creation*. Macmillan, 1964.

Maier, Norman R. *Problem Solving & Creativity in Individuals and Groups*. Brooks/Cole Publishing, 1970.

Maynard, Fredelle. *Guiding Your Child to a More Creative Life*. Doubleday, 1973.

McKim, Robert H. *Experiences in Visual Thinking*. Brooks/Cole Publishing, 1972.

Mooney, Ross L. ed. *Explorations in Creativity*. Harper & Row, 1967.

Osborn, Alex F. *Applied Imagination*. Scribner's, 1957.

Osborn, Alex F. *Your Creative Power*. Scribner's, 1949.

Parnes, Sidney J. and Harding, Harold F. ed. *A Source Book for Creative Thinking*. Scribner's, 1962.

Prince, George M. *The Practice of Creativity*. Macmillan, 1972.

Raudsepp, Eugene. *Creative Growth Games*. Jove, 1977.

Rosner, Stanley and Abt, Lawrence E. ed. *The Creative Experience*. Grossman, 1970.

Rugg, Harold. *Imagination*. Harper & Row, 1963.

Torrance, Ellis P. *Guiding Creative Talent*. Prentice-Hall, 1962.

Young, James W. *A Technique for Producing Ideas*. Crain Books, 1975.

8 AN INDEX OF POSSIBILITIES

Do as many or as few of these creative games
and exercises as you like; or, make up your own.
But remember, the only way to develop any skill
-- and that includes creativity -- is through
practice.

You can read this section in five minutes or
less; to finish it may take a week or more. Flip
the pages slowly, like index cards. Stop and
listen to each idea before going to the next.
Consider these exercises to be an index of your
own creative possibilities.

1. Imagine where and what you'll be doing exactly
   two months from today. Imagine a weekend in the
   summer of 1989. Imagine your home in 1992.
   Write an entry in your diary for tomorrow.

2. Take 12 index cards and write a single adjective
   on each, such as white, triangular, fuzzy, etc.
   Be specific rather than general. Now, shuffle the
   cards and deal the top two. List as many objects
   as you can that possess these two attributes.
   Continue through the deck.

3. Break one comfortable habit every day for a week. Change your daily routine. What happens?

4. Create for yourself a do-nothing period that lasts five minutes or two hours. Do nothing and see what happens.

5. Close your eyes and recall ten distinct smells, such as the smell of freshly cut grass or burnt feathers. Keep each smell in mind for a few minutes and notice what you associate with each. Go to the spice rack and sniff one spice after another (make pepper last). Do any of these smells provoke memories you thought you'd forgotten?

6. Browse through an antique shop or read an old magazine looking for *new* ideas.

7. Gather a number of old magazines, a pair of scissors, and some rubber cement. Relax your inhibitions. Now, cut out three images that appeal to you and create a dream scene. Use four images to express an emotion such as anger. Use five images to create a cartoon, and then caption your creation.

8. Imagine putting your problem on a lazy susan in front of you. Revolve it slowly to get a view from all sides. Now, imagine yourself suspended overhead. Examine the problem calmly and with curiosity.

9. The next time you jog or go for a walk, identify twelve different colors; smells; sounds.

10. Solve a problem with your feelings. Ask yourself
    what kind of solution would make you feel happy;
    inspired; reflective; proud; guilty?

11. Begin a creative notebook. Write down your
    observations, questions, insights, whatever,
    about the problems you want to solve creatively.
    Use the notebook for list-making, free
    associating, brainstorming; sketch in it. Ask
    yourself periodically "how am I doing?" and
    give yourself feedback.

12. Make a habit of asking "what if?"; for example, what if you lived somewhere else? what if you worked at home? what if you were married or divorced? what if you had six months to live?

13. Stand up and look between your legs for two
    minutes.   Is anyone watching?   If so, this
    exercise is doubly effective: two people are
    gaining a new perception of their surroundings.

14. When confronted with a problem, set an arbitrary number of ways to define it; for example, three or five or seven. Then, set another number of solutions and ideate until you've reached your quota.

15. Let yourself drift into a daydream. Put your mind into a canoe and let it float downstream. What happens?

16. Imagine you have been given a color television, a videotape machine, a home computer, a 35 mm camera with all the lenses, a tape recorder, a stereo with AM-FM radio. Now, realize you already own all of this: it's called your mind.

17. Try Leonardo da Vinci's technique for new ideas:
    "I have seen in the clouds and in spots on a wall
    what has aroused me to fine inventions."

18. Imagine a deck of cards in your hands. Pick out the jacks with one eye; the king with the raised sword; the queen facing right. Now, get out a real deck of cards and examine the face cards carefully.

19. Spend an hour on a distant hill with a pair of
    binoculars. Roll up this book and scan the room
    for several minutes. Look into your backyard
    through the bottom of a glass.

20. Encourage yourself to be creative. Encourage your friends and children, too. This book is only a primer to creativity -- a book of first principles. Whatever you do, don't stop here.

Relax and have fun. You can't be
creative if you're always too serious.